ONEX
No Ordinary Dog

Debi K Stinson

Copyright © 2025 by Debra K Stinson
All rights reserved. This book or any part of it may not be reproduced or used
without the express written permission of the publisher,
except for the use of brief quotations in a book review.
Printed in the United States of America
First Printing, 2025
ISBN 979-8-9892641-7-9

To our beloved Onex.

We miss you, buddy.

ONEX
No Ordinary Dog

Table of Contents

1 No Ordinary Dog..1

2 A New Beginning..5

3 The Copperhead Encounter........................7

4 A New Mission..11

5 A Lifesaving Bond..15

6 Stepping Forward..19

7 Fetch?..23

8 Making a Splash..29

9 A Well- Earned Rest.....................................35

10 Fire in the Night...39

11 The Aftermath..43

12 Rebuilding and Healing............................45

13 A New Place, A Familiar Comfort.........49

14 A Hero's Final Journey..53

15 Last Act of Unconditional Love...............................57

Chapter One
No Ordinary Dog

From the moment Onex was born, he had a job to do. That playful little puppy didn't know the adventures he would experience or the impact he would have on so many people. The sleek black Labrador Retriever with sharp instincts and an unwavering focus was trained at Lackland Air Force Base in San Antonio, Texas. He was to become an Explosive Ordnance Disposal (EOD) dog.

The training was tough, but Onex was tougher. He learned to detect explosives, navigate chaotic environments, and work alongside soldiers in the field.

After graduating from extensive training, he deployed to the Middle

East, where his skills saved countless lives. For three years, he searched for hidden dangers, his nose always working, his mind alert. There was no time to play, only duty. But, like all soldiers, Onex's military service eventually ended. He retired from the Army and was shipped back to the United States. That's when his life took a new turn.

Chapter Two

A New Beginning

When he came back, Onex was adopted by an elderly Navy veteran in Tennessee. The man gave him something he had never experienced before—freedom. No more strict commands and no more endless work.

For the first time, Onex could simply relax.

He took naps on the couch, went on long walks, and savored his food. Life was good. But Onex's instincts never faded. When danger came, he was ready.

Chapter Three
The Copperhead Encounter

One summer morning, Onex and his owner took their usual walk down a wooded path on a friend's farm. The world felt peaceful, but in an instant, that peace shattered.

A copperhead snake lay curled up on the path ahead, its eyes locked on them. Before his owner could react, Onex lunged forward, placing himself between the snake and the man he loved. The snake struck—once, twice—its venom sinking into Onex's face and chest.

It hurt, but Onex stood his ground. Memories of his military training kept him calm in the face of danger. Onex staggered, his body growing weak. His owner didn't hesitate. He scooped Onex into his arms, rushing him to the car and speeding toward the nearest veterinary hospital.

For days, Onex remained at the hospital, fighting off the venom. His owner was awaiting the moment his loyal companion would wake up, tail wagging. When that day finally arrived, the man knew one thing for certain—Onex was meant for something greater.

Onex made a full recovery, wearing the scars on his face and chest as badges of honor.

Chapter Four
A New Mission

Knowing that Onex still had more to give, his owner made a difficult but selfless decision. He enrolled Onex in the Train a Dog Save a Warrior (TADSAW) program, where he would be retrained as a service dog for a veteran in need.

It wasn't easy. Onex, once a soldier, then a carefree pet, had to relearn discipline. After months of training, he was paired with Retired Sergeant First Class Chris Stinson, a disabled veteran who had returned home from war carrying invisible wounds.

Chris had suffered a traumatic brain injury (TBI) and battled post-traumatic stress disorder (PTSD).

Loud noises made his heart race, a feeling that Onex knew all too well, and seizures sometimes struck without warning. He needed a partner—someone who would watch over him, sense when something was wrong, and bring him back from the darkness.

Onex was that partner.

Chapter Five
A Lifesaving Bond

Onex took his job seriously. As other dogs in the household played, he remained at Chris's side. He enjoyed stomping his feet as if performing a river dance, a habit that made his new owner laugh.

One afternoon, Chris was in the garage working on his truck when he became dizzy. Onex sensed something was wrong. A second later, Chris collapsed.

Onex didn't hesitate. He sprinted to the gate, barking frantically to get the attention of Chris's wife, Deb. The moment she stepped outside, Onex turned and ran back toward the garage, leading her straight to him. She immediately called an ambulance.

Onex refused to leave Chris's side, standing guard as paramedics arrived. When Chris finally woke up in the hospital, he saw Onex curled up beside his bed, his tail thumping gently against the floor.

"You saved me, buddy," Chris said, scratching behind Onex's ears.

Chris never took Onex for granted. He wasn't just a service dog — he was family.

Chapter Six
Stepping Forward

Chris sat on the porch, his eyes fixed on the horizon. The scent of fresh-cut grass filled the air. Beside him, Onex lay stretched out, basking in the sun.

It had been a long road. The darkness that once gripped him had loosened its hold, little by little, thanks to the steady presence of the black lab at his side.

Chris gently petted Onex and said, "You have been my rock, buddy."

Onex's tail gave a gentle thump as if to say, *I know*.

Chris took a deep breath. His seizures had become less frequent. The nightmares weren't as relentless. For the first time in years, he felt...

capable. The idea of returning to work—something he had once thought impossible—no longer felt out of reach.

"I think it's time," he said, his voice steady. He looked down at Onex, who lifted his head, ears perked. "Time to go back, to do more than just survive."

Onex let out a huff. He had carried Chris through his hardest days, guiding him through the shadows, and now Chris was ready to step forward on his own.

He cradled Onex's face, looked into his eyes, and said, "I couldn't have done it without you."

Onex nuzzled into his hand. As they stared at each other, he was reminded of all they had overcome together.

Chris stood, stretching, feeling the weight of the past lift a little more. The future didn't seem so daunting.

Chapter Seven
Fetch?

With Chris returning to work, Onex now spent his days with Deb and his fur siblings. Deb stood in the grass with a bright yellow tennis ball in hand.

"Alright, Onex," she said, "go get it!"

She tossed the ball across the yard. It bounced several times, then rolled to a stop. Onex just sat there. His ears perked, his head tilted slightly, but he didn't move. Fetch? That wasn't something he had ever done. He was trained to work, to follow orders, to search and protect—not to chase silly things.

Jake and Corey, his fur brothers, had no such hesitation. They bolted after the ball. Jake snatched it up first, trotting back with his tail wagging.

Onex watched.

Deb laughed. "Come on, Onex, give it a try."

The next time she threw the ball, Jake and Corey took off again, barking with excitement. Onex's eyes followed them, his body tensing. Something inside him stirred—an unfamiliar itch in his paws.

The ball bounced.

Jake and Corey ran.

And this time… Onex ran, too.

He wasn't as fast as Jake, and Corey nearly beat him, but it didn't matter. The wind rushed past his face, his paws pounded the earth, and for the first time, he felt it—pure, simple joy.

When the ball was thrown again, he didn't miss a beat. He chased, he ran, he jumped. He even caught it once, feeling victorious, before Jake playfully stole it back.

Deb clapped. "That's it, Onex, good boy!"

His tail wagged wildly. At that moment, he was just a dog, free to run, to play, to enjoy every moment. It felt amazing.

Chapter Eight
Making a Splash

The sun beamed down as the dogs chased the tennis ball across the yard. Onex was fast. He had learned the game now, and he loved it.

Deb tossed the ball, but this time, when the ball bounced, it didn't stop. It rolled…and rolled…until—*plop!*

It splashed into the pool.

Corey launched himself into the pool, paws first, making a huge splash. Onex skidded to a stop at the edge, watching. His eyes followed Corey as he paddled effortlessly toward the floating ball.

Then, as if an invisible force took over, he jumped in.

Splash!

Cool water wrapped around him, but instead of panicking, he felt weightless. His paws kicked, his legs moved, and suddenly, he was swimming.

As soon as his paws hit the pool steps, he scrambled out, tennis ball in tow.

Onex bolted across the yard, soaking wet, ears flopping, tail wagging, and ran straight to Deb.

He dropped the tennis ball before her and pressed his face against hers, planting a big, wet kiss.

She laughed as she wiped the water from her face.

"Oh, Onex!" She giggled, wrapping her arms around him. "I love you."

Onex just wagged his tail, tongue hanging out. He had discovered something new—he loved swimming.

And he couldn't wait to do it again.

Chapter Nine
A Well- Earned Rest

As the years passed, Onex's body grew weaker. Diabetes took its toll, and eventually, he lost his eyesight. But even in darkness, Onex never lost his spirit. He continued to move with confidence, guided by the sounds and smells around him.

He finally retired as a service dog. He spent his days lounging on the porch, listening to squirrels rustle in the trees and soaking up every belly rub he could get.

One afternoon, Chris sat beside him, petting him. "You're a great boy, Onex," he whispered. "I don't know what I would do without you."

Onex didn't need to see him to know how much he was loved. He simply sighed in contentment, resting his head against his best friend's leg, knowing he had fulfilled every mission life had given him.

Except one…

Chapter Ten
Fire in the Night

The fire started silently. A spark, a flicker—then flames spreading through the walls. Thick smoke curled under the doorways, creeping into every corner of the house. The Stinson family slept soundly, unaware of the danger.

But Onex knew.

The scent of smoke jolted him awake. His ears twitched, and his nose flared as he sprang to his feet. A piercing alarm blared through the house, shrieking over the crackling flames. Onex barked loudly, urgently and desperately.

The air was thick, burning his throat as he ran from room to room, barking frantically. The other dogs were awake now, their whimpers and barks mixing with the growing panic. Footsteps pounded against the floor.

"Get out! Get out!" Deb screamed.

The fire moved fast. Smoke turned the air dark. Dogs scrambled, their nails skidding against the floor as they ran in confusion. Chris coughed, his mind sluggish from the smoke, but Onex stayed close, pressing against his legs, guiding him out of the house.

Flashing red and blue lights filled the night as fire trucks and police cars arrived. The roar of water being sprayed against the blaze echoed through the air, but the fire raged on.

Then, just as quickly as it began, it was over. The house was gone.

When the last fire truck pulled away and the night finally fell silent, all that remained was the brick fireplace where Onex had once loved to lay, now standing alone in a pile of ash.

Chapter Eleven
The Aftermath

The days that followed felt like a blur. The family moved through the motions, their hearts heavy with loss. The weight of six missing fur siblings pressed against them, an absence that could never be filled.

But through it all, Onex remained their anchor. Because of him, three adults and five of their beloved pets escaped with their lives.

As Chris sat beside Onex, he whispered, "You saved us, buddy. Again."

Onex didn't need words to understand. He leaned against Chris, his tail thumping softly. No matter what they lost, they still had each other.

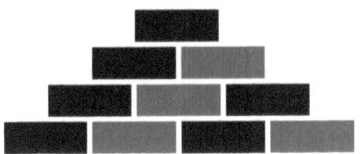

Chapter Twelve
Rebuilding and Healing

The year that followed the fire was sad. The echoes of their old life lingered. The Stinson family struggled with their loss; the familiar walls that once held laughter and warmth were gone, reduced to ash.

Onex felt it, too. He wandered through their temporary home, his paws searching for the familiar creak of old floorboards and the scent of his fur siblings, who were no longer there. He sensed the sadness in his family, their whispered words, their tired eyes. He curled up beside them each night, offering silent comfort, his presence a reminder that not all was lost.

There were days when the darkness seemed unending, but slowly, light began to seep back in. The sound of hammers and saws outside became a promise of new beginnings.

Brick by brick, their new home took shape. Onex would listen from a distance. He knew change was coming, new smells, new corners to explore, and new memories to make.

When they finally stepped into their rebuilt home, it felt different—strange yet familiar. Onex made his way through each room, reclaiming it as theirs. As they unpacked boxes, hung photos, and settled in, the shadows of grief slowly lifted.

Life began again, not the same, but moving forward. Together, they started building new memories stronger than before, held together by the unbreakable bonds they had forged in the fire.

Chapter Thirteen
A New Place, A Familiar Comfort

Onex stepped onto the porch of their new home; something felt right. The boards were sturdy beneath his paws, and warmth from the afternoon sun caressed his face. A gentle breeze carried the familiar scent of pine and earth.

He took slow, careful steps, and his nose lowered as he traced the edges of the porch. It wrapped all the way around the house, giving him space to wander, to feel, to listen. The birds still sang their familiar songs, and the squirrels still rustled in the trees. Onex let out a deep sigh and lay on the wooden floor. It wasn't the same as before, but it was good.

A hand reached down, scratching behind his ears. Deb said, "You like it, buddy?" Onex thumped his tail against the floor.

Yes. He did.

Onex rested his head on his paws, feeling the love of his family. He knew this was home.

Chapter Fourteen
A Hero's Final Journey

Onex enjoyed the last few years of his life with his family. In his final moments, his body was tired, but his heart was full. He lay peacefully surrounded by his family. They pet him and spoke of love and gratitude, reminding him of all the years that he had spent loving and protecting them.

Deb held his paw, her voice cracking with emotion as she told him what a good boy he was, how much he had done for them, and how he would always be their hero.

The room was quiet except for the sound of sniffles and murmured reassurances. His family told him stories of his bravery—how he saved them from the fire, how he had always watched over them, how he had always been their constant source of comfort and protection.

They assured him it was okay to go. They knew he was tired. He was always so strong for them, and it was time for them to be strong for him. He had lived his life with purpose.

Onex let out a gentle sigh as if he understood, like he was saying his own goodbye.

As the weight of exhaustion settled over him, he felt only love. He had done his job, and now it was time to rest. As he took his final breath, the room was filled with both sorrow and gratitude. They would grieve for the loss of their beloved companion but also celebrate the incredible life he had lived.

Onex, their hero, will never be forgotten.

Chapter Fifteen
Last Act of Unconditional Love

As the family sat on the porch in reflection, Chris whispered, "We miss you, buddy." There was a pause, a deep breath and then, just for a moment, they heard it: the gentle rhythm of tapping feet, the unmistakable sound of Onex's river dance.

Bittersweet smiles crossed their faces as they wiped away their tears. "You're still here, aren't you?"

The breeze shifted, wrapping around them like a familiar embrace, and at that moment, they knew Onex had never truly left.

His love, his loyalty, and his spirit will always be with them.

Author's Note

Service dogs, like Onex, play a vital role in helping people with disabilities and medical conditions live fuller, safer lives. These highly trained animals assist veterans with PTSD, guide individuals who are blind, detect seizures before they happen, and even provide emotional support in times of distress.

Programs like TADSAW, work tirelessly to match service dogs with veterans in need, creating life changing partnerships. The bond between a service dog and their handler is built on trust, love, and loyalty— something that cannot be replaced.

If you would like to learn more about service dogs and the incredible work they do, consider visiting organizations who train and support them. These dogs are more than companions, they're heroes.

For more information about TADSAW visit: https://tadsaw.org

About the Author

Debi K Stinson, author of the Fuzzy Pickles series, was born and raised in Royal, Alabama and lives in Clarksville, Tennessee. She is a graduate of the University of Alabama. She enjoys spending time with her family and working on her farm, Little Legacy.

Her passion has always been children, animal rescues, and giving back to her community.

Reading Comprehension

1. What was Onex trained to do at Lackland Air Force Base?
2. How did Onex save his owner from the copperhead snake?
3. What program did Onex join after retiring from military service?
4. Describe how Onex helped his owner, Chris, when he collapsed in the garage.
5. What happened to Onex during the fire in the night?

TN Man Saved From Snake By Ex-Military Dog

Author: Gannett News
Published: July 24, 2012

CLARKSVILLE, TENN.- During a routine stroll on a friend's farmland off Peachers Mill Road, a 70-year-old man found himself face-to-face with a copperhead snake.

Luckily, he had a fellow veteran with him: Onex, a black Labrador not afraid of a fight.

Navy veteran Darrell Layne said that on July 14 he was opening a large cattle gate on the farm, but an old rotted fencepost blocked the gate. After he moved it, the fencepost broke in two. He threw one of the pieces aside, then noticed the venomous snake at his feet.

"I'm looking down, and not far was a copperhead," he said. "He was coiled up and ready to strike me."

Layne said he doesn't normally see copperheads in the area, but there's an old rock bluff where they might embed themselves.

"I know a copperhead when I see a copperhead," he said. "He was 20 inches long, and he was a deadly snake."

Nearby was Layne's 5-year-old dog Onex, who served the Army in the Middle East before landing in Clarksville in November.

"This dog was trained in Iraq," Layne said. "He was trained to sniff ordnance and possibly other things; he was a rescue dog too."

Layne said he lucked out receiving Onex with dog tags because of the dog's Army background.

"I was very lucky to get him," he said. "It wasn't your normal adoption."

When Onex saw the snake threatening Layne, he crouched forward growling, which diverted the snake's attention. But now the attention was on Onex, and the snake bit the dog twice on the face.

That gave Layne the opportunity to grab a fencepost and kill the snake.

Onex was in bad shape though. Layne had to rush him to the veterinarian, where the dog was treated for two days with fluids and anti-venom.

"I would have never got out of there," Layne said. "He got real sick on me before we got back to the truck."

"In this particular incident, he knew exactly what to do," he said. "I'm 70 years old, and I'm not as strong as I used to be."

Layne said he and Onex have become closer since the incident.

"He's very protective of me, and I've noticed this more since this happened," he said. "I know what could have been if I didn't have him."

The dog's head remains swollen from the bites, but a full recovery is expected, Layne said. "Dogs can be the best partner you have, and unconditional love describes Onex," he said. "People need to take care of their pets like they would their best friend."

Onex and Mr. Layne

PHOTOS

The day Onex joined the Stinson family

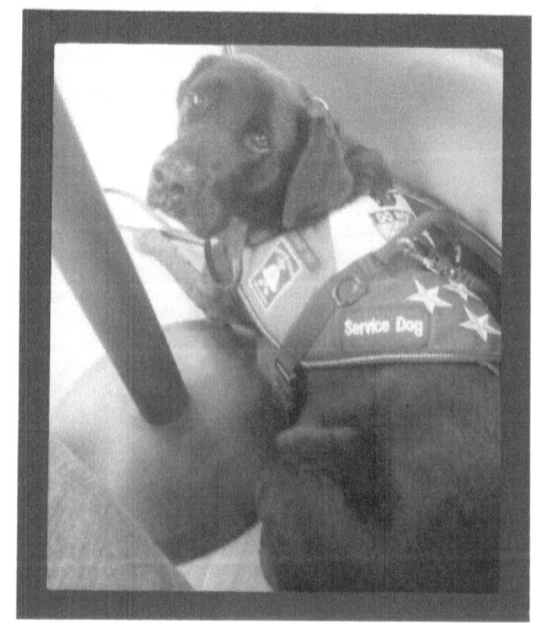

Onex at a restaurant with his family

Chris and Onex after they graduated from the TADSAW program

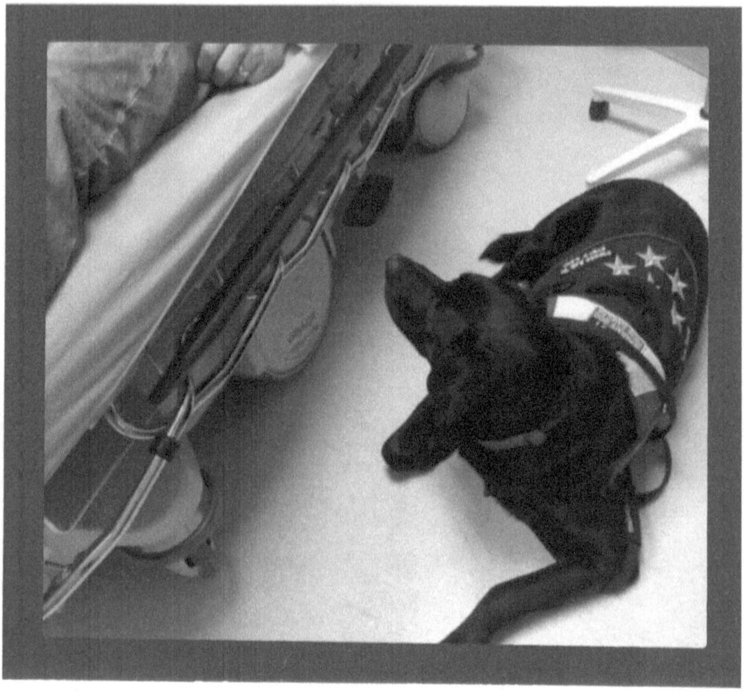

Onex next to Chris's hospital bed

Onex giving Chris kisses

Onex, Corey, and Jake playing tug-of-war

Onex learning how to use the doggy door

Campbell, Layla, and Onex

Onex at his sister's wedding

Onex swimming

Onex with his tennis ball

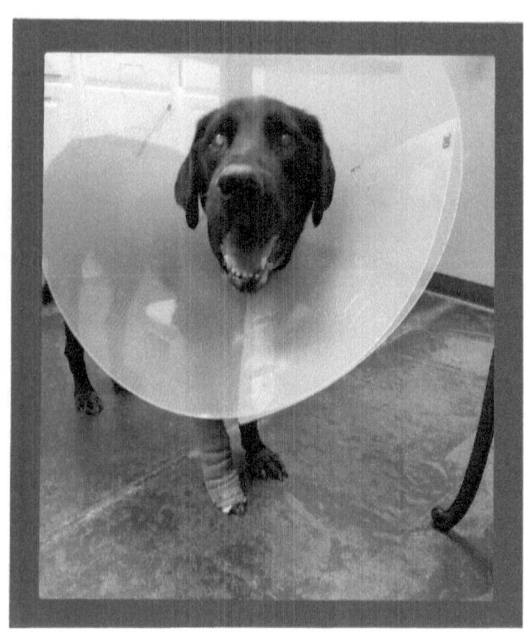

Onex at the vet

Jake and Onex by the fireplace

Onex and Jake in front of the Christmas tree

Deb and Onex at Christmas on the Cumberland

Onex in his Christmas sweater

Deb, Onex, and Jake with Santa

MWD Fun Facts

- As of 2025, there are approximately 2,700 active duty military canines serving in the United States armed forces.[1]
- Since Robby's Law passed in 2000, all military dogs are eligible for adoption after their term of service.
    - 90% of military working dogs (MWDs) are adopted by their handlers.[2]

---

[1] www.37trw.af.mil
[2] www.saveavet.org/robby-law-reports

- Dogs have served in the U.S. military since the Revolutionary War.[3]
- There are several U.S. War Dogs Memorials.
- Nonprofits like Mission K9 Rescue and Patriot K9 Rescue help find homes for retired military dogs.
- The order of priority for retired MWDs is usually the former handler, other military veterans, and then the general public.

---

[3] https://porchpotty.com/blogs/news/military-dogs

- Sergeant Stubby, a dog who served during WWI, is said to be the most decorated war dog. His many awards include two purple hearts.[4]

---

[4] calvetconnect.blog/2021/08/06/phr-who-risked-their-hides/

Did You Know?

- Service dogs are highly trained professionals.
- Service dogs can be any breed or gender.
- Service dogs can assist people with many different types of disabilities and can be trained to perform a wide variety of tasks.
- Under the Americans with Disabilities Act (ADA), service dogs are permitted access to places where pets are not allowed. These places include, but are not

limited to, hospitals, restaurants, and schools.
- Dogs are generally the only animals recognized as service animals under the ADA, however, in some rare circumstances, miniature horses can qualify.

Service Dog Etiquette

- Service dogs should never be separated from their handlers.
- Always speak to the handler and not directly to the service animal.
- Never touch a service dog without permission.
- Do not distract a dog when they are working. Distractions could potentially endanger the dog's handler.

Onex
2007-2020

Our beloved Onex passed away March 16, 2020 at Animal House Veterinarian Hospital in Clarksville. He was 13 years old.

Onex valiantly served his country in Iraq from 2008-2011 as a trained bomb sniffer for the U.S. Army returning to the states in November 2011.

Onex was adopted by a senior Navy veteran. On a walk with his new owner, they approached a copperhead snake ready to strike. Onex immediately went into action to save his owner and was bitten twice. Onex survived the attack after days of treatment. Onex's owner knew that he was an extra special canine and wanted to bless another veteran that needed a service dog.

Onex came into our lives in 2013 through TADSAW, Train a Dog Save a Warrior. Onex was trained to be my husband's service dog. My husband suffers from PTSD, TBI, as well as other disorders caused by an IED. Onex has saved my husband's life many times over through his skills and bravery.

Due to his declining health, Onex finally retired in 2016. He spent his retirement enjoying the fine things in life: cookies and love. Lots and lots of love.

Onex was and will remain a big part of our family.

In Loving Memory

Norabella   Campbell   Mia

Charley   Gypsy   Layla

July 19, 2018

FOLLOW US
Let's Connect

SCAN ME

www.ingramcontent.com/pod-product-compliance
Lightning Source LLC
Chambersburg PA
CBHW030452100526
44580CB00006B/95/J